START A BUSINESS

THE A TO Z OF STARTING AND RUNNING A SUCCESSFUL SMALL BUSINESS

Peter Osalor

Table of Contents

INTRODUCTION

Success is not partial. No matter your location, race, religion, age, size, or color. If you want to succeed, you must make the choice to succeed; it is a decision. All the successful people on earth follow the same principles and practices to succeed. Success is predictable, it is based on principles and if you follow the principles you will succeed. Do what successful people do and you will succeed.

We are living in the best times now because of information technology. Information and knowledge are very, very easy to access. Behind them lays an explosive competition where people are trying to move forward, further, faster. The competition is more creative and aggressive than ever before. It is like a business war; the dog eat dog era. You cannot afford to be ignorant in the 21st Century or it will cost you greatly.

Every failure can be linked to a lack of knowledge and understanding. Most businesses that failed do so because they engaged in the same practices that made them fail.

Running your own business has become more necessary in the 21st century due to the economic down turn in 2010 and unsecure jobs. There are not enough jobs for people anymore and in many cases, mass unemployment is everywhere. In the BRIC nations and MINT nations the economic growth rate is up to 7% – but it is between 1 to 3% throughout the rest of the world.

Large companies have collapsed or downsized – this has encouraged governments to set policies that encourage the establishment of small businesses. All of the above factors have made starting your own small business very necessary. It is one of the best ways to employ yourself and create jobs.

You must be open minded, and know that your success depends on you and no one else. You must also be willing to work hard, learn new principles and unlearn others, you must be willing to embrace advancements in technology, and realise that your success depends on you.

What are principles?

The *Business Dictionary* defines principles as:

Fundamental norms, rules, or values that represent what is desirable and positive for a person, group, organization, and help in determining the rightful ness or wrongfulness of its action.

Principles can also be defined as: "Elementary assumption, concept, doctrine, maxim, or proposition generally held to be fundamental or true for a body of knowledge, conduct, procedure or system of reasoning".

Principles are more basic than policy and objective – they are meant to govern both. Principles have been tested and proven right, and once you abide by them, you won't go wrong.

In this book, you will discover the principles that successful businesses are built on. Most successful businesses, and people, are where they are today because they choose to abide to these principles. So, if you want to succeed all you have to do is continue reading.

My story

My background is not what you would call inspiring. I was born in Warri in 1955 and my parents were petty traders. My father was always in-and-out of menial jobs and we never had any money. I started fending for myself from the age of 8. Once I left primary school, there was no money to send me to college but I eventually managed to get into a college as a house boy. After college, I started working. With little education, I worked my way up and eventually secured a position in Kano with Panalpina World Transport. In March 1983, I left for London to study to become Chartered Accountant became a Tax Adviser 1991 and by June 1992, I opened my own practice, Peter Osalor & Co.

My practice attracted only MSMEs which were okay; I had some plc. clients but not really large ones. Since 1992, I have had over 3000 clients and most of them have ceased trading. Some went into liquidation and some just seemed to disappear into the thin air. I became worried and started asking questions and researching the possible cause. I soon discovered that the businesses that were no more failed because of the same reasons and the ones that survived, survived because they applied the same principles. It is those principles that I wish to share with you because in order to create a successful small business your venture must abide within them. These principles of a business are the driving force that makes successful businesses successful. They are the backbone of every great organization – big and small.

The principles work irrespective of who you are and where you are. They are like a phone number, no matter how intelligent you are, how sincere you are, how determined you are, if you dial the wrong number – you will not get through.

Be pragmatic; if something works, apply it and do it. Your success rests on the extent to which you apply what works – wherever and whenever appropriate.

This book will give you the 'a to z' of starting and running a successful business, as well as 26 irrevocable principles for business success. The smartest people in this world are those who take the time to find out the rules of success in an area, before they attempt to get results in that area. Always apply the 10/90 percent rule:

10% of your time is invested in finding out the facts and planning.

90% of your time is invested in the execution and achieving the goals.

Principles are neutral; they are indifferent to your personal beliefs, preferences or desires. They have always existed and will always will. Principles are always true and always right – the faults and errors are always ours. (Johann Wolfgang vin Geothe).

My favorite book, the holy book, says that people perish because of ignorance. Ignorance costs, and ignorance kills. Go and search for the truth – and the truth that you know and apply will set you free.

Remember that ignorance of the law is no excuse. If you are ignorant of the law of gravity – you will still experience its effects if you jump off a bridge. Even if you do not know the principles you will still experience the consequences of them.

Before we go into the nitty - gritty, you must be absolutely clear in your mind about what you would like to accomplish by owning your own small business. Answer the following questions and be meaningfully specific rather than answering generally:

- What are your values?
- What do you believe in and stand for?
- What is most important to you in life?
- What would you pay for, fight for, suffer for, and die for?
- If you had only one hour to live, what would you do?
- What is your vision for yourself? (answer this question in relation to your future, your family and finances, your career and your business)

Peter Drucker said, even if you are starting your business on a kitchen table, you should have a vision of becoming a world leader or you will never be successful. Think big – there is nothing wrong with aiming high!

Here are some additional questions for you to ponder on:

- What is your mission?
- What do you want to accomplish for your customers?

You must have a clear vision and mission to motivate you.

- What is your life's purpose?
- Why did you get up this morning?
- What is your reason for being?

Your goal must be clear.

- What would you dare to dream of, if you knew you could not fail?

You must be ready and willing. You must also be competent in your choice of business, and passionate about it. Know the constraints, be creative, concentrate, focus, and be fearless. The ultimate reward, according to Jim Rohn, is that your greatest reward in becoming a millionaire or becoming successful is not the amount of money that you earn. It is the kind of person that you have become, to reach success in the first place. You must become more to have more; you must develop to a 'high-quality' person to obtain 'high-quality' results.

You must have practiced the principles of clarity, competence, creativity, concentration and consistency until they all become natural to you.

Should something happen and you lose everything, you will be able to make it all back again because you have transformed – you have become different. The truly successful person has not forgotten what he did to become rich; success can be repeated because it has become part of them – that is the true spirit of an entrepreneur. So, you see it is a fun, exciting journey and it is worth it.

This book will be divided into three parts:

   A. Before you start

   B. How you start

   C. Sustaining, growing, and exit plans

Let us now enter chapter one where we shall discuss the part "A" conditions that are prerequisite to starting your business.

CHAPTER ONE

Part "A"

(Before you start)

"There are no secrets to success. It is the result of preparation, hard work, and learning from failure." **Colin Powell**

THIS CHAPTER COVERS:

- It starts from the mind
- Do you have what it takes to be an entrepreneur?
- Entrepreneur aptitude test
- What makes an entrepreneur?

The business starts from the mind

Success starts in the mind and so should your business. But you have to take consistent action and ensure you are moving toward what you want, but getting the power of the mind behind your dreams is critical and easy. If you are mentally ready for a business then you must dream it, because if you can't dream it, you can't achieve it. The business idea starts right from your mind, it has to be first conceived and be pre-planned in your mind before it can become realizable.

There's the old adage that when the Why is compelling enough, the How will show itself. On some levels that's partially true. But, unless you've taken the time to understand what you value about your dreams and what you believe to be true, the unconscious mind will only show you the how that aligns with your picture of reality based on your past.

Humans are bombarded with over two million bits of information at any given time. Yet, our mind spectacularly filters the onslaught of data we receive so our senses won't be overwhelmed. It's like we have an internal colander, if you will, and the holes allow the right information to seep through based on your definition of important as seen through your memories, desires, values, attitudes, behaviours, and beliefs. From there, it compartmentalizes further by taking that data and putting it into perceived associations and themes so your conscious receives just seven pieces of data, give or take a few.

Every plan and process starts from the mind; if you cannot think it you cannot do it.

Do you have what it takes to be an entrepreneur?

There is an enormous difference between wanting to do something and being able to make a living at doing that something. Have you ever watched the American Idol audition shows and witnessed a tone-deaf singer's shocked reaction when the say he or she will never have a shot at becoming a professional singer? The same thing can be true for entrepreneurship.

Being a successful business owner requires investing your own money in addition to a ton of time and effort. Despite the appeal of being your own boss, the reality is that not everyone is cut out to be a successful business owner.

Here are five quick personality assessments to evaluate before taking the entrepreneurial plunge:

Are you Santa or an elf?

Entrepreneurship requires managing a wide variety of tasks as part of the business, from marketing and accounting to training, customer service and more. Can you wear multiple hats, as Santa does with Christmas, or do you prefer to be the elf that loves to execute specific tasks? Do you take initiative or do you want clear instructions? Santa makes better entrepreneurs than elves do.

"Entrepreneurs adopt the ways of the adept and adapt to a changing environment. Actually, entrepreneurs are more enter-preneurs, because they are forever entering into new territory."- **Jarod Kintz.**

What's your relationship with money?

Starting a business requires money to start, to operate and for you to live on while it scales. If you are a big spender and aren't great at managing money, those bad habits are likely to follow you into a business. And if you are usually unable to make worthwhile investments in the future of your business for fear of ending up living in a cardboard box if things go wrong then you may end up penny wise and pound foolish, as they say. Having a solid, non-emotional money relationship will help you make wise business decisions.

The man who will use his skill and constructive imagination to see how much he can give for a dollar, instead of how little he can give for a dollar, is bound to succeed. **- Henry Ford**

Are you comfortable flying blind?

The only thing that is certain in business is that nothing is certain. Are you comfortable with being uncomfortable? Can you handle taking educated risks and surviving the constant ups and downs of owning a business? If you are looking for the certainty or a drama-free zone, you may find yourself terrified of the entrepreneurial roller coaster.

"You know you are on the road to success if you would do your job, and not be paid for it." - **Oprah Winfrey**

Are you ready to commit?

Running a successful business is not just about having great ideas. It's more about strong execution. So, if you have a hard time staying focused, you are lousy with commitments and you're averse to the idea of working day in and day out on the same thing, then entrepreneurship may just be a passing fancy for you.

To be successful, you have to have your heart in your business, and your business in your heart. **- Thomas Watson, Sr.**

Were you born for business?

Were you interested in business as a child? Did you seek out entrepreneurial roles in school, in social organizations or even in your previous job? A natural inclination of past interest in entrepreneurship seems to be a good potential indicator of future success.

Think you're cut out to be an entrepreneur? Or are you still unsure? Take this informal quiz to see how your answers compare with the popular profile of today's successful entrepreneurs.

Evaluate your strengths and weaknesses

It's rare that one person possesses all the qualities needed to be successful in business. What's important is to understand your strengths and weaknesses. To do this, you need to evaluate the major achievements in your personal and professional life and the skills you used to accomplish them. The following steps can help:

1. **Create a personal resume**. Compose a resume that lists your professional and personal experiences as well as your expertise. For each job, describe the duties you were responsible for and the degree of your success. Include professional skills, educational background, hobbies, and accomplishments that required expertise or special knowledge. When it's complete, this resume will give you a better idea of the kind of business that best suits your interests and experience.

2. **Analyze your personal attributes.** Are you friendly and self-motivated? Are you a hard worker? Do you have common sense? Are you well-organized? Evaluating your personal attributes reveals your likes and dislikes as well as strengths and weaknesses. If you don't feel comfortable around other people, then a business that requires a lot of customer interaction might not be right for you. Or you may want to hire a "people person" to handle customer service.

3. **Analyze your professional attributes.** Small-business owners wear many different hats, but that doesn't mean you have to be a jack-of-all-trades. Just be aware of the areas where you're competent and the areas where you need help, such as sales, marketing, advertising and administration. Next to each function, record your competency level—excellent, good, fair, or poor.

In addition to evaluating your strengths and weaknesses, it's important to define your business goals. For some people, the goal is the freedom to do what they want when they want, without anyone telling them otherwise. For others, the goal is financial security.

Setting goals is an integral part of choosing the business that's right for you. After all, if your business doesn't meet your personal goals, you probably won't be happy waking up each morning and trying to make the business a success. Sooner or later, you'll stop putting forth the effort needed to make the concept work.

When setting goals, aim for the following qualities:

- **Specificity.** You have a better chance of achieving a goal if it is specific. "Raising capital" isn't a specific goal; "raising $10,000 by July 1" is.
- **Optimism.** Be positive when you set your goals. "Being able to pay the bills" isn't exactly an inspirational goal. "Achieving financial security" phrases your goal in a more positive manner, thus firing up your energy to attain it.
- **Realism.** If you set a goal to earn $100,000 a month when you've never earned that much in a year, that goal is unrealistic. Begin with small steps, such as increasing your monthly income by 25 per cent. Once your first goal is met, you can reach for larger ones.
- **Short and long term.** Short-term goals are attainable in a period of weeks to a year. Long-term goals can be for five, 10 or even 20 years; they should be substantially greater than short-term goals but should still be realistic.

There are several factors to consider when setting goals:

- **Income.** Many entrepreneurs go into business to achieve financial security. Consider how much money you want to make during your first year of operation and each year thereafter, up to five years.
- **Lifestyle.** This includes areas such as travel, hours of work, investment of personal assets, and geographic location. Are you willing to travel extensively or to move? How many hours are you willing to work? Which assets are you willing to risk?
- **Type of work.** When setting goals for type of work, you need to determine whether you like working outdoors, in an

office, with computers, on the phone, with lots of people, with children, and so on.

- **Ego gratification.** Face it: Many people go into business to satisfy their egos. Owning a business can be very ego-gratifying, especially if you're in a business that's considered glamorous or exciting. You need to decide how important ego gratification is to you and what business best fills that need.

The most important rule of self-evaluation and goal-setting is honesty. Going into business with your eyes wide open about your strengths and weaknesses, your likes and dislikes, and your ultimate goals lets you confront the decisions you'll face with greater confidence and a greater chance of success.

Entrepreneur aptitude test

PROGRESS STATUS:

Mark to select your option. These questions will help you understand and discover more about yourself. They will also help you if you desire to be a successful entrepreneur

1. I am easily discouraged when I encounter obstacles.
2. I am very imaginative.
3. I feel restricted in situations where I am expected to follow strict rules and codes of conduct.
4. I like figuring out how things work and why.
5. I enjoy being in a position of authority over a group.
6. My family supports my ideas, no matter how outrageous they seem.

7. I have a hard time finding motivation to myself beyond my limits.
8. I have a high-energy level
9. I thrive on change.
10. I am optimistic.
11. I feel confident about my abilities.
12. I want to make lots of money.
13. Getting to know people makes some happy.
14. I break promises.
15. I have difficulty adjusting to change.
16. I perform well under pressure.
17. I can come up with a creative solution for most problems I encounter.
18. I strive to fill the needs of people.
19. I have a high-energy level I am obsessed with amassing wealth.
20. People seem uncomfortable around me.
21. I have certain characteristics that make me special.
22. I believe that you have to take risks to be successful.
23. When I have great idea, I immediately take the initiative to get the ball rolling.
24. I get excited about trying new things.
25. I bounce back quickly from personal or professional failure.
26. I am able to apply what I've learned to different situations.
27. I'm able to influence the opinions of others.
28. I like to read books or articles about.
29. Innovative business people.
30. I am confident that my friends are Looking-out for my best interests.
31. I am comfortable instructing others.

32.   I excel at brainstorming different ways to reach goals.

33.   When something goes wrong, I feel like the world is ending.

34.   I don't have a strong support system of friends.

35.   Selling things or ideas to others is easy for me.

36.   I have the ability to create my own opportunities.

37.   I generally expect that the outcome of situations will be favourable.

38.   I have close relatives who have been successfully self-employed.

39.   I can easily build a good rapport with people

After you have completed the aptitude test, give it to an already established entrepreneur or your mentor or a professional entrepreneurial organization to evaluate your performance and give you professional advice on the business you have in mind to start.

Let us now see what makes an entrepreneur

What Makes an Entrepreneur?

Entrepreneurs have a greater capacity for pain and discomfort than others. They can stay up later, work longer hours, stay more focused and, somehow, are able to set so much aside in deference to their dreams and visions. But there's so much more that sets them apart.

Statistically, the average UK entrepreneur is a 36-year-old white male working in the construction industry. But statistics can be very misleading. Because in fact, successful entrepreneurs and business owners come in absolutely all shapes and sizes: aged between 9 and 109, male, female, rich, poor, people with multiple doctorates and people who left school at 13, and they are from every ethnic background you can think of. What they have in common is the drive to make things happen.

I have found no greater satisfaction than achieving success through honest dealing and strict adherence to the view that, for you to gain, those you deal with should gain as well. **- Alan Greenspan**

This guide explains the personality traits that make entrepreneurs who they are. And if the below sounds like you, you could well make a great one!

Determination

- Starting and running a business is incredibly hard work and is usually riddled with complications, frustrations and constant set-backs.
- You have to be determined to succeed to pull yourself through these obstacles.
- You also have to be ready to put in incredibly long hours, every day of the week, for months - if not years.
- Determination is also what will keep you searching for the best contracts and deals for your business, or that one material you just can't seem to find - which often takes hundreds of phone calls for days on end.
- It's also vital for forging commercial partnerships with the people you want to - your perseverance will prove a lot about you and encourage others to trust in your ability.
- It is only with determination that you will plough on trying to find the business model, marketing technique, and sales strategy to make your business a real success - as these things can take years to refine and perfect.
- If you're not determined to make your business a success, you need to seriously question whether starting up is right for you.

Confidence

- You've got to have confidence to be able to get through the hard times. And there will be hard times: when you're working 14-hour days, it looks like you've just lost your life savings, and you're still not getting any customers. You need deep emotional reserves and inner confidence in yourself and your business idea to get through that.
- Confidence also enables you to approach the people you need on-side: commercial partners, lucrative clients, target customers, suppliers.
- It also reassures them that you know what you're doing, and so encourages them to work with you.
- Confidence will be an invaluable asset in any pitch or presentation you have to make.
- If you doubt your own confidence, fear not - there are ways to improve it. Try one of the multiple self-help books or website tutorials out there aimed at improving esteem.

Action-orientated

- Ideas are absolutely worthless unless you do something about them. You need to be a go-getter to make any aspect of your business happen.
- Entrepreneurs are the kind of people who just get on with things, rather than sitting around talking about them.
- You need, though, to be able to structure to your action. Just leaping in for the sake of it is foolish - you need to have clear paths of action to make a business idea a reality.

Passion

- Being passionate in business doesn't mean that you're a fiery, emotional, romantic hot-head - it means that you truly believe in the business you're building, that the idea behind it excites you, and that when you talk to people about what you're doing, it's obvious you're really into your new business and determined to make it work.

- Passion for a business idea - and the ability to communicate it - is what gets staff, investors, banks, customers and commercial partners interested in your idea.
- It can be fantastically convincing, and will always help you strike deals and bring in custom.
- It is also your passion that will motivate staff and suppliers when times are tough - you need to inspire them to keep working hard to make things happen.

Ability to see the bigger picture

- When you're running your own business, you'll face constant setbacks.
- You need to the kind of person who can see the bigger picture so these don't get you down.
- You also need to view finances, strategy and growth from a more holistic point of view so you can plan years into the future - as all businesses should - rather than just weeks or months.
- This is invaluable for your budgeting and business planning, and, so, for the survival of your business.

People person

- Business is all about relationships.
- To be successful, it'll really help if you're the kind of person who can build rapport easily and isn't afraid to strike up a chat.

- You also need to build a relationship with customers and make them want to do business with you because they like you.
- When people like you, it also increases their loyalty to your business - a crucial tool to help pull you through the darker times, or when a new competitor starts up just around the corner.

Risk-taker

- The very best entrepreneurs, with strings of companies and millions in the bank, are almost always the biggest risk takers. Without risk, there is no reward.
- That means grabbing an opportunity when you see one and not being afraid of failure.
- That said, entrepreneurs take calculated risks - which their actions may look flippant, you can rest assured that they're doing the maths inside their head to always make sure they've got a high chance of succeeding if they take a risk.
- Only a fraction of business owners become full-blown entrepreneurs - the type who run hundreds of businesses all across the world. But you can take inspiration from them, by trying to always remember to push yourself and your ideas that little bit further.

Not afraid of failure

- If you worry too much about failing, you'll never start a business. You have to be willing to fail if you want to succeed.
- Banishing a fear of failure also gives a massive boost to your confidence and risk-taking ability - after all, if the worst option isn't to be feared, you might as well have a go.

- You need to try to banish fear not just of your business failing, but also of an important contact turning you down or a client deciding not to do business with you. If you're always worried about this, it will stress you out far too much and make you seem much less confident.
- And remember - you learn best from your mistakes in business. Don't fear them - embrace them!

Opportunity-spotter

- Key for being able to identify market gaps, new customers, new product possibilities and, if you become a fully-fledged entrepreneur, new business opportunities.
- Opportunity-spotting often comes hand-in-hand with optimism - and the ability to take calculated risks.
- It'll help you find more inventive sales, PR, marketing and partnership ideas too.
- If you think this area needs work, start noticing how big companies are spotting new opportunities - how they capitalise on trends and target their advertising. And start reading books on how businesses have developed in new and creative ways.
- You'll know if you're an opportunity-spotter if you're always coming up with ideas or you often see how products and business could be more efficient or more popular.

Financial thinker

- Entrepreneurs always think of profits and the bottom line. If you're not focused on making money or at least breaking even, you're not going to have a business for very long - just a cash-drain.
- Being able to calculate figures quickly will help, but it's not imperative. What is vital is that you always remember to

work out costs and profit margin on everything you buy and
sell and add or deduct it from your budget.

- Thinking through any financial decision carefully is far more
important than doing so quickly.

Frequently Asked Questions

What if I don't think I have all these traits? Can I still run a
business?

The guide is just a round-up of the most common entrepreneurial
traits. But some very successful businesspeople are painfully shy,
and some perfectly competent business owners never take risks and
aren't too hot in the maths department either. However, if you feel
that you lack most or all of these personality traits, you might want
to think about whether you're really ready to start a business now, or
whether it would be better to try to develop your skill-set for a few
years first so you know you have the best shot at things when you do
eventually start.

We now move to the next chapter where we shall answer the
question" why do you want to start your own business.

CHAPTER TWO

WHY DO YOU WANT TO START A BUSINESS?

"Character cannot be developed in ease and quiet. Only through experience of trial and suffering can the soul be strengthened, ambition inspired, and success achieved." - **Helen Keller**

THIS CHAPTER COVERS:

- Why do you want to start a business?
- The advantages and disadvantages

Running your own business has a tendency to take up most of your life, so it's vital to assess whether or not your reasons are solid. This chapter looks at some of the most common reasons for people to start their own business, the pros and cons of each, and the best path forward.

"If you really want to do something, you'll find a way. If you don't, you'll find an excuse." - Jim Rohn

Do you have a killer idea?

- If you really have landed on a great idea that satisfies a market need for a substantial number of customers, you have the potential to really fill a niche and establish a business quickly and effectively.
- A brilliant idea is also contagious - something exciting and original will interest other people, so you're more likely to draw in investors and customers.
- Be aware that lots of people believe they have fantastic business ideas, only to realise there's no real market for their business, someone else has done it already or the product of

their imaginings is too difficult or expensive to actually manufacture.

- You need to do incredibly thorough market research if all you have is an idea at this point.
- Every product or service has to fill a market gap and have. Make sure yours does.
- You also need to be very careful about patents and other intellectual property (IP).
- Make sure your idea doesn't infringe on anyone else's IP. Check the patent database.
- Is there any part of your idea you can copyright? You'll probably have to start playing around with creating it first to find out. You'll want to patent whatever you can so it can't be copied by competitors. But bear in mind most patents take at least six months to come through, and they're difficult to obtain.
- Be very aware of the financial viability of your idea. Work through everything that would be involved in its manufacturing to see if there is actually any room for profit.
- You might think your idea is great, but the hard work hasn't even begun yet. Don't go off registering your business just yet, taking your time and figuring out the details is your next step.

Do you have Passion for your business?

- If you absolutely love what the business you want to start does, you're going to work far harder - which you'll need to if you want to make it a success.
- Your enthusiasm will also be very appealing to investors and customers.
- You're likely to understand your target customer much better if you know your field well, so your marketing efforts have a better chance at success.

- You also need to be aware that just because you're working in a field you're passionate about, it's not all going to be fun and games, there's going to be a load of admin and boring stuff to get through, which will take up most of your time.
- You also need to make sure you have a deep understanding of your subject, not just a superficial interest, to make your efforts worthwhile.
- You still need to do extensive market research, particularly into the size of your target market and whether other people like you would want your business' service of product offering.
- Read books on market research for more information.

Do you want to be your own boss?

- The idea of answering to no one but yourself will always be attractive, but in reality, the added responsibility and time it takes can be a far cry from the dream.
- If you're going to start up in the industry you're currently working, you could make things easier for yourself as you'll already have the market knowledge and contacts necessary to make your business work.
- Just make sure you don't infringe any competition clauses laid out in your contract.

Necessity

- Starting a business is hugely rewarding.
- It also fills a gap you might not otherwise have on your CV - whether or not your business is long-term or successful, it will prove to future employers that you have driven, you were willing to broaden your business experience and take a risk, and you will have gained invaluable skills you wouldn't have if you'd only been job-searching.

- It will also help prevent the pains most people get when they can't find work.
- If you're struggling to get into the industry you want to career-wise, starting a business in it can prove you have the skills, determination, experience and commitment further down the line and open up more job opportunities as a result.
- Don't commit too much money to a business you're not planning to run in the long-term.
- On the other hand, this might end being a business you stick with for life - so it's well worth doing things properly. This will also teach you a lot more than a haphazard approach.

The challenge

- If you're starting your own business because you want a new challenge, you won't be disappointed!
- It tests a huge variety of skills and you'll learn loads along the way.
- You'll also meet plenty of like-minded people and get to know your market really well.

Make a million

- If you start with a plan to make a million pounds, don't hold your breath. While new people become millionaires every day, bear in mind they have put in a huge amount of hard work.
- If your business hits the rocks, you are less likely to be motivated enough to steer it out of trouble if your sole intention was to make money. It's often better to find an idea you are passionate about.
- Making a million is not impossible - but for that to be your sole aim, you usually need to be someone who is very financially minded with a natural knack for business.

- You may well have been showing signs of entrepreneurialism all your life - selling to kids in the playground, to friends and family. Using holidays to do small business, sell to friends.
- You still need to approach a business in the same way as anyone else - careful research, planning, getting the funding in place and rigorously testing your idea before taking it to market.

Ideas alone are not enough - you need to have something tangible and new to be able to protect it legally. It takes more than an idea to make things happen, and it takes more than talent to get to the top. We now see the necessary actions before you convert the idea to a business.

Before You Convert That Idea to a Business

To be a successful business owner it requires investing your own money in addition to a ton of time and effort. Despite the appeal of being your own boss, the reality is that not everyone is cut out to be a successful business owner.

"In order to succeed, your desire for success should be greater than your fear of failure." - **Bill Cosby**

The Effects of Owning Your Own Business

Many people dream of owning a business and see it as a way to control their own destiny. Starting a business is an exciting venture that offers many benefits. However, you should also analyze what it takes to run a successful business. Although no special skills are required, running a successful company takes determination, patience and an understanding of business principles. Not fully understanding the advantages and disadvantages of owning your own company may hinder your path toward successful entrepreneurship.

Salary potential

When you work for an employer, you know your annual salary and little opportunity is available to earn more money on your job. Starting your own business gives you the potential to earn a high salary, you can define your own income base on your contribution. Productivity, pricing and marketing plans are all under your control, and the income you earn relates to those activities. Although earning a high salary is not a guarantee, the potential to earn a lucrative income is available.

Do what you enjoy

Owning a company gives you the opportunity to work in a field you enjoy. Working in an industry you're passionate about helps you better handle down times in your business. Owning your own business allows you to create and contribute, which gives you personal satisfaction. Most entrepreneurs working in a field they enjoy also bring their expertise, which allows them to offer innovative products and services to customers.

Business control

Entrepreneurship gives you the control over your business. If you operate a sole proprietorship, you make the final management decisions regarding your company. Some individuals thrive in situations where they experience independence. Owning a business gives you the power to control how active you are in the business. You can participate in every step of the decision-making process, or you can hire competent people to make decisions in the best interest of the company.

Demanding work schedule

Many business owners work long and erratic hours, and some people view this as a disadvantage. Work schedules are the most gruelling for new business owners, because they usually handle time-consuming administrative tasks. The responsibility of running the business ultimately rests upon your shoulders, so you may experience days when you need to stay in the office until the task is complete.

Financial risks

A disadvantage of owning a business is that you must incur financial risk. Whether you used your own savings or borrowed money for start-up costs, the money invested in your company is at risk. Some companies go out of business and cause business owners to lose their initial investment or default on business loans. Even with a solid business plan, economic volatility can cause your business to lose money and eventually close for good.

Liability

Depending on your business structure, creditors and customers may possess the ability to seek your personal assets if you default on your business obligations. If a customer or vendor believes you acted in error, he may file a lawsuit against you. To protect your company's assets, you can seek liability insurance for your business, but some new business owners may find it difficult to afford insurance premiums.

The impact of your business to the economy

It is a reality that SME's are the backbone of most developed countries, in the British economy, producing a major contribution to the GDP in the UK. In 2013 SMEs employed 14.4 million people (over half of all employees) and had a combined turnover of £1,600 billion (nearly 50% of the total turnover of business in the UK). The government is claiming to be business friendly by removing a lot of bureaucracy and red tape (excessive regulation) to encourage small businesses to thrive. Of course, we are all aware that financing start-up businesses and getting investment for a growing business is still a challenge in the current economic climate.

So, if you are already a business owner, or are you considering becoming one, then you should make sure that you are fully informed of the advantages and disadvantages of business ownership.

Owning and running your own business can be exciting and rewarding, but it brings with it a number of factors that you will not have experienced as an employed person. As a business owner, when all the work you put in starts to bring results it can be exhilarating and lucrative, however you should be aware of the risks as well as the benefits.

Advantages of being your own Boss

As a business owner, you are in charge and accountable only to yourself, you answer to no one and you make all the decisions. You can work as many hours as you wish and use your time for work or leisure without having to seek permission to take time out. Depending on the type of business, you may be able to work anywhere (home, office, coffee shop, pub etc.).

You can often control your own income and focus on the type of work that you enjoy and not be accountable to others who may force you to engage in activities that you feel are non-productive or non-essential.

Flexibility and freedom

As a business owner, you have the ability to choose the jobs you wish to undertake, choose the clients you wish to work for and decide when and where you wish to work. That is not to say that as a business owner you can necessarily work just a few hours per week, it is more about choosing when you wish to work.

You are not restricted by process and can potentially delegate or outsource the boring mundane tasks and concentrate on the creative elements of the business. This will become a very important aspect of running your own business as it evolves, often the business owner will be sucked into daily dross and lose sight of the strategic vision.

Agility

As a business owner, you are able to become aware of opportunities and initiatives that you can pursue quickly without having to seek permission from your bosses. You can put your own ideas into practice, this will become a massive plus as a small, agile business often wins against the apathetic corporate mentality of larger organisations.

Be passionate with what you do

A business owner will often start a business because they are passionate about what they do. This will create vitality and enthusiasm that will be infectious and will attract potential clients who want to work with you. You will want to get up every day and make a difference, your energy levels will be high and your passion will carry you through the day.

Create your own persona

As a business owner, you can use a number of business titles depending on your audience or target market. Titles such as Owner,

Principal, Proprietor or Managing Director can create different identities for you.

The title can be a valuable asset should you wish to close your business and seek further employment as you can claim experience based on your title.

Disadvantages of being your own Boss

Owning a business can expose you to financial risk. You may have to go into debt or invest substantial personal funds to start your company, any business growth normally requires extra investment.

Lack of concrete planning

As a business owner, you need to plan ahead and ensure that the investments you make are in the right areas. Seek proper advice before you make the extra investments, there may be a better and less expensive method of achieving your desired outcome.

Do not be content after you have made the changes, ensure that you review and measure and confirm that the changes are beneficial. It is not a weakness to change or even discard ideas if they are not bringing the required benefits.

Long working hours

You may have to work long hours in the early years, often for less pay than anticipated while the income goes to meet operating costs, which may include a payroll, administration, marketing, operational activities. You may not be able to take a reasonable holiday in the early days.

If you have belief and passion in what you are doing then in the short term you will have the energy to work longer hours to succeed. As the business develops and grows start to look at the strategic view and consider working with an external consultant or adviser to get a dispassionate view of your business to ensure you are on the right track. This can include a re-structuring of your business by promoting staff internally to take on some of the vital tasks or even looking to recruit a supervisor or manager.

A lot of energy can be expended worrying about your future plans or anxiety may kick in if you are unsure. An external ear can be a vital component to keeping you focussed and positive.

Lack of vision

Once your business is established, its income may be sporadic, highly variable or seasonal. Ensure you carry out a cash flow forecast for 3, 6 and 12 months. Be realistic about the future of the business, looking at worst case and best case scenarios, do not get caught having to cover unexpected shortfalls.

Develop a realistic vision for the business, keep re-visiting this and ensure you are focussed and driven.

Lack of strategy

Operating a business on your own entails dealing with many facets and details. You may spend most of your time tending to the business instead of doing the work that you enjoy. You may get sucked into spending a lot of time working in the business on minutia rather than being strategic and growing the business.

You may have to learn new disciplines such as bookkeeping, market research, employment law, general administration. Although at the time this can appear to be tiresome and unnecessary it will give you the ability to ensure that when you delegate the roles you can be clear about the responsibilities and the key performance indicators.

Undertake a time management exercise to ensure you are focussing on the important aspects of the business and your personal development. Make sure you spend quality time in the top right hand quadrant to develop and grow your business.

Time management

In simple terms, spend most of your time focussing on the important aspects of the business – like planning, meeting deadlines, meetings, relationship building, personal development, preparation. Do not get sucked into the unimportant activities, you may feel you are working hard but actually you will be achieving very little. You can delegate administrative work and accounting work, employ the right person to fit in these positions, administrative work and accounting work is as important as building business network.

It can be a lonely place

When the business is going well and thriving you will have vitality and focus. However, during periods of discontent and negative growth you may need support (emotional and material) to keep focussed and continue with your trust in the business. It may not be appropriate to lean on your family or friends as they will support you, but they will not be able to give the concrete advice and reassurances that an external adviser or consultant will be able to provide.

Conclusion

Being your own boss is exciting and rewarding, however it can be a short-lived dream and cause distress and upset if it goes wrong. To reduce the possibility of failure, make sure you research the key areas of your market and spend time continually educating yourself in the disciplines of running a business. Seek expert help from accountants, marketing specialists and business advisers, you will receive invaluable support and probably realise 'you didn't know what you don't know' and be able to develop a realistic plan for your business.

Small businesses are the life blood of the British economy and many other developed economies. As a business owner you deserve immense respect for stepping out of the safe environment of the corporate world and providing employment for others. The risks you take deserve the huge rewards that can be achieved in status, finance and prestige. A successful business owner can continue to enjoy the fruits of his labour or could deploy an exit strategy that will give them a rich and rewarding retirement.

We now move to chapter three where we shall discuss your business Ideas and how to achieve it.

CHAPTER THREE

Part "B"

(How you start)

How to achieve your business Ideas?

"You have to be burning with an idea, or a problem, or a wrong that you want to right. If you're not passionate enough from the start, you'll never stick it out."— **Steve Jobs**

THIS CHAPTER COVERS:

- Your business idea, will it fly?
- Market survey and research

In the previous chapter, I talked about having a killer idea, having a good product or service idea that will break the ground. All this begins with a thought and starts from within; it is from the inside that you make the decision to start a business. Now you must ask yourself, "What type of business should I venture into?"

You already know that there's a world of possibilities out there for anyone who wants to start a business. How can you possibly know and find the type of business that's right for you? The approach outlined will help. Once you've worked your way through these five decisions, you will have a much better idea of what type of business you want to start.

Types of business

Retail or wholesale type of business?

Where do you want to be positioned on the supply chain? Retail businesses sell goods directly to consumers, usually in small quantities. Wholesalers buy goods (often in large quantities) from manufacturers or importers and then sell them to retailers and other distributors.

Franchise or independent type of business?

Many established companies offer franchises, which are basically copies of their companies. If you buy a franchise, you are buying the right to sell the parent company's goods and/or services in a specific area. Besides paying a franchise fee, you will also have to pay royalties and perhaps additional fees to the franchisor. You will also be expected to abide by the terms of the franchise agreement, which will often lay out exactly the way you will do business. Buying A Franchise explains the advantages and disadvantages of franchises and what to expect.

An independent business is one that you create and nurture on your own. Starting an independent business allows you the control and freedom that you won't get from a franchise operation.

Product or service (or mix of both) type of business?

If you are a trained professional, such as a dentist, accountant, agriculturist or realtor, your business is going to revolve around the professional services you can provide. But there are many professionals that also have the opportunity to offer related products, if they choose to do so.

If you're a photographer, for example, you may decide to sell cameras, picture frames, and photo paper.

If you're not a trained professional, the key to deciding whether to focus on products or services when you're thinking about starting a business is determining where your true talents lie and what you most enjoy doing. Would you be happiest telling someone how to do something, doing something for them or offering them the products they would need to do the job themselves?

DO NOT base this decision on whether or not you enjoy selling or are good at it. No matter what type of business you start, you will be involved in sales.

Storefront or non-storefront type of business operation?

Winnowing through business opportunities and finding the right business to start becomes much easier when you know exactly what you're looking for.

If you have decided to start a business selling products, you need a storefront of some kind, whether bricks-and-mortar, such as a retail store, or virtual, such as an e-commerce site. Many successful businesses have both, expanding their customers beyond their locale. Others "borrow" a storefront, so to speak, by getting their products distributed by other businesses, selling their products through markets and fairs, or by using available e-commerce venues. (Selling on eBay is one example of this.)

If you have decided to start a business selling services, you may or may not want a storefront. Many different services are actually performed at a customer's home, from cleaning through landscaping. While you would still need an office (either in your home or elsewhere), an actual storefront is unnecessary.

Some services can be offered over the phone or the Internet, such as the services offered by virtual assistants or some business coaches. These businesses often depend on virtual storefronts (business web sites) to attract clients. You can build a website that works and will even expand your client's base.

Another option is to use your home as a storefront. There are many other services that can operate successfully as home-based businesses, from travel agents through hairdressing, (hairdressing, barbing saloon, car wash and many more simple service business can be done by rendering Home service to your clients).

In which industry/topic?

To make it easier on yourself, choose an industry or topic that you are not only interested in but have some expertise or experience. Otherwise, you're going to have to spend a lot of time and money educating yourself that you could be putting into your new business, or worse, making costly mistakes because you don't have the necessary knowledge.

To figure out if you should go ahead with your business idea, you also need to ask these following questions like these.

- Is the market saturated? Is there room in the market for one more business?
- Is there a demand for your particular product/service?
- What are the competitions doing? What do they do well? What do they do poorly? What is unique about them?
- Can you offer something different that will encourage customers to patronise you instead of more established businesses?
- Can you reach your target audience?

Your Winning Type of Business

Now you're ready to look for a business that fits the bill. Suppose, for instance, you've decided that you want to start a business that's retail, independent, product based, has a storefront and is related to gardening. Then the businesses that you might start (or look to buy) would include nurseries, garden shops, or a business specializing in gardening-related products, such as greenhouses or hydroponic equipment.

You can see that this still gives you a really broad range of choices, but has narrowed these choices down to the types of businesses you are most interested in owning or operating, as opposed to wandering through the whole bewildering array of possibilities.

Once you've broken it down this far, it's time to let research be your guide, searching for the "matching" business opportunities in your area, and if none exist, doing the market research that will show you specifically what type of business in the topic area or industry you're interested in has the most potential.

How to Research Your Business Idea

Your brilliant idea may indeed be brilliant--or it may need some work. Here's how to find out whether you're ready for start-up.

Somewhere between scribbling your idea on a cocktail napkin and actually starting a business, there's a process you need to carry out that essentially determines either your success or failure in business. Oftentimes, would-be entrepreneurs get so excited about their "epiphanies" (a sudden intuitive leap of understanding, especially through an ordinary but striking occurrence) the moments when they imagine the possibilities of a given idea-that they forget to find out whether that idea is viable.

Of course, sometimes the idea works anyway, despite a lack of market research. Unfortunately, other times, the idea crashes and burns, halting a business in its tracks. I like to help you avoid the latter. These steps will teach you how to make a market survey and offer tips for optimizing your results.

The idea stage

For some entrepreneurs, getting the idea-and imagining the possibilities-is the easy part. It's the market research that doesn't come so naturally. It's a big red flag when someone outlines the size of the market-multibillion dollars-but doesn't clearly articulate a plan for how the idea will meet an unmet need in the marketplace, (Identify of the needs that are yet to be met in the market and use it as an opportunity to make a difference).

That kind of full-throttle approach can cost you. Entrepreneurs are often so passionate about their ideas, they can lose objectivity. Rather than taking the time to thoroughly plan and research, they sometimes plow ahead with execution, only to spend valuable dollars on unfocused or untargeted activities."

Market research, then, can prove invaluable in determining your idea's potential. You can gather information from industry associations, Web searches, periodicals, federal and state agencies, and so forth. A trip to the library or a few hours online can set you on your way to really understanding your market. Your aim is to gain a general sense of the type of customer your product or service will serve-or at least to being willing to find out through the research process.

Your research plan should spell out the objectives of the research and give you the information you need to go ahead with your idea, fine-tune it or take it back to the drawing board. Create a list of questions you need to answer in your research, and create a plan for answering them. Utilize experts in planning and conducting research sessions. They can recommend what type of research is most appropriate, help you develop statistically valid samples and write questionnaires, and provide you with an objective and neutral source of information."

The type of information you'll be gathering depends on the type of product or service you want to sell as well as your overall research goals. You can use your research to determine a potential market, to size up the competition, or to test the usefulness and positioning of your product or service. "If, for example, the product is a tangible item, letting the target audience see and touch a prototype could be extremely valuable, for intangible products, exposing prospective customers to descriptive copy or a draft Web site could aid in developing clear communications."

Analysis

When working with firms on brand development, first looks at a business idea from different perspectives: company, customer, competitor and collaborator. This approach will allow you to scrutinize a business idea before even approaching the topic of brand development. Here's what he looks at for each of the four issues:

1. Company. Think of your idea in terms of its product/service features, the benefits to customers, the personality of your company, what key messages you'll be relaying and the core promises you'll be making to customers.

2. Customer. There are three different customers you'll need to think about in relation to your idea: purchasers (those who make the decision or write the check), influencers (the individual, organization or group of people who influence the purchasing decision), and the end users (the person or group of people who will directly interact with your product or service).

3. Competitor. Again, there are three different groups you'll need to keep in mind: primary, secondary and tertiary. Their placement within each level is based on how often your business would compete with them and how you would tailor your messages when competing with each of these groups.

Competitors' analysis

- The key to winning market share is to differentiate your company by providing products, services or solutions that your best prospects will find more desirable than what's offered by your closet competitors.
- The job of convincing qualified prospects to buy from you instead of your competitors is where real works begins.

These simple four step competitors' analysis will help you in analysing your competitors.

1. Do some detective work
2. Evaluate "perceived "competitors
3. Focus on the message
4. Find a unique spin

4. Collaborators. Think of organizations and people who may have an interest in your success but aren't directly paid or rewarded for any success your business might realize, such as associations, the media and other organizations that sell to your customers.

Another approach to research is SWOT analysis, meaning analysis of the strengths of your industry, your product or service; the weaknesses of your product (such as design flaws) or service (such as high prices); and potential threats (such as the economy). "[SWOT] enables you to understand the strengths and flaws, [everything] from internal information such as bureaucracy, product development and cost to external factors such as foreign exchange rates, politics, culture, etc. SWOT enables an entrepreneur to quickly understand whether their product or service will make it in the current environment.

Whatever your approach to evaluating your idea, just be sure you're meeting the research objectives you've outlined for your product or service. With those goals always top-of-mind, your analysis will help you discover whether your idea has any holes that need patching.

Checking out the competition

Assuming your research process has helped you uncover your competition, you now need to find out what they're up to. Become a customer of the competition, whether by shopping them yourself or by enlisting the help of a friend. Visit their Web site and put yourself on their list. Talk to your competitor's customers, ask them what they like or don't like about your competitor's product or service. If you conduct formal research, include a question like 'Where do you currently go for that product or service and Why?

Your aim is to understand what your competition is doing so you can do it better. Maybe their service is poor. Maybe their product has some flaws-something you'll only know if you try it out yourself. Or maybe you've figured out a way to do things better, smarter, more cost-effectively. Find your selling point. It's going to be the core of your marketing program, if and when you're ready for that step. It's also going to be what sets you apart and lures customers your way.

When Your Idea Looks Like a Flop

After all this, the idea stage, analysis of the idea, competitive analysis you might find out that your idea (and not your competitor's, as you'd hoped) is the one with the holes. Does that mean you need to scrap the whole thing and resign yourself to life as an employee? "NO," all you need to do is just needs to be reworked or retooled, don't give it up.

That can be disheartening if you've already spent hours in the idea stage, plus huge amount of hours on market research only to find that you're not quite ready to get it started after all. But taking the time to refocus your energies and determine why your idea needs some tightening is the best predictor of future success. Ask yourself, 'Is this a weakness that can be overcome?' If you can't create true value for your customer and your business, then it's time to pick another idea to pursue.

Remember, ideas simply need some fine-tuning. Before you panic and start flipping through your idea books again, closely consider whether you can make this idea work. After all, there was a reason you thought of that idea in the first place. Some ideas that seem like they'll be total duds after doing a little research end up being great successes. "Ideas that seem like a flop are always interesting and high chance of success. Sometimes you look into an idea and find it was just luck but many times, you find the original founder had some clear insight into the potential. That insight was his or her focus, and it seemed to lead them to success.

When Your Idea Is Good to Go

The market research you've conducted thus far ought to be a good indicator of where you need to go next with your idea. One key factor to consider is pricing. You want to do it competitively while also considering what the market will bear. For products or services that have a close competitor, I will advise choosing an attractive price, moderate enough to make the customer concentrate their interest on the quality of product or service that is, pricing with respect to the competitive position.

The beauty of being in business for yourself is that you have the option to make changes at will, so if a pricing structure isn't working, you can alter it. Make sure your price is not too low and not too high, make sure is the best price at the quality.

You need to be sure that your product or service is delivering enough, make sure everyone that use your product or service will want to continue to do business with you. Set value that will justify the price you set. If possible, test different pricing offers as you go, and determine what works best.

When you're ready to get started, be sure you are selling where your target market is likely to buy. Your marketing plan and budget should include a well-crafted distribution strategy. If you'll sell or render service over the Internet, budget for media to drive new customers to your site. If you'll sell via retail distribution, you might need workers with industry experience to help you reach your target market.

Remember, too, that you can always seek help in this long, arduous process of bringing an idea to fruition. The Internet, your local library, the Census Bureau, business schools, industry associations, trade and consumer publications, industry trade shows and conferences, and new-product development firms can be invaluable sources of information and contacts. It's just a matter of seeking knowledge from as many sources as possible. It's also a matter of putting your ego aside and being willing to create a business that will not only survive, but thrive. If you have an idea, don't be afraid to refine it, re-organise it, re-think it continually. The more you do that before you launch, the less you'll have to do afterwards, and the less painful the lessons tend to be.

Market surveys are an important part of market research that measure the feelings and preferences of customers in a given market. Varying greatly in size, design, and purpose, market surveys are one of the main pieces of data that companies and organizations use in determining what products and services to offer and how to market them.

How to conduct market research online

Whatever the size of your business, market research surveys give you a quick, affordable way to perform market segmentation analysis. Find out key demographic information on consumers in your market. Then use surveys to do just about anything, from measuring customer satisfaction to developing new products. There are lots of ways Survey Monkey can help. Get a jumpstart by trying an expert market research survey template that is reliable.

The only way to keep your customers, or gain new business, is to know exactly what consumers want. Guesswork and gut instinct won't cut it when it comes to launching successful products and crafting the right marketing messages.

HOW MARKETING PROS USE ONLINE SURVEYS

Reach a specific audience

Surveys offer a great opportunity to get input from your target market – provided you have good market sample to send surveys to. Maybe you have a customer list or a big group of social followers to work from. If you don't, Survey Monkey Audience gives you access to millions of respondents who are ready to provide the answers you need. By sending a survey to members of your target market, you can make sure your efforts will be as effective and reliable as possible.

Update product offerings or pricing

Sending an online product feedback survey to customers will help you gain insights that drive product improvements, customer satisfaction, and ultimately, sales. To get product feedback, you will ask questions like: what changes would most improve our new product? Or, what do you like most about competing products currently available from other companies?

Build social media strategies and campaigns

With the increasing importance of social media in many companies' marketing mix, online social media surveys are a great way to figure out which social media channels they need to pay attention to. Likes and retweets only tell you so much. Surveys help you understand the "why" and give you ideas for how to serve your market. Post marketing surveys on Facebook or Twitter to gauge interest in new product categories or features. And should you send out company updates via a blog, LinkedIn, or Facebook? Use an online survey to find the answers you need.

Research and analyze a target market

Your marketing budget is probably one of your business's largest expenses. Before you earmark funds for any marketing plans or initiatives, you need to be confident that the strategies you're considering will drive your success. A market research survey can help you analyze the potential market size, find a prime location for your retail store, or the optimal price for your products. The effort you expend on a market study will be rewarded with go-to-market strategies that have a higher chance of success.

Gain insights into customer demographics

Need to identify potential customer demographics in a new service area? Ask potential customers about their gender, age, location, income, where they shop, what they do for fun, how many children they have, and more. You can then target your messaging and campaigns to really speak to your customers. You'll also be able to concentrate time and resources on where they'll matter most.

Market segmentation

Segmenting your customers, that is, homing in on smaller groups that shares common attributes (such as demographics, geography, lifestyle, product usage, brand affinity etc.) might just help to tip the scale in your favor. To gain this competitive advantage, many marketers send online surveys.

A health club owner could segment based on facility or service usage (spa, cardio equipment, daycare, nutrition classes), while a consumer packaged goods company might segment based on lifestyle (health-conscious, low-cal, vegetarian diet) to develop finely tuned marketing programs that target the needs of one or more of the segments in order to increase membership sign-ups. When you do market research, it's easier to identify different segments and know what they want.

Decide which campaign creative to launch

Would your customer base be more likely to respond to an online banner ad or a billboard on the freeway close to home? Which email subject line would make you click through to the product detail page? Do you need to test a new ad format? Helping to prioritize ad spend and resources, online marketing surveys should be an essential tool in your strategy toolkit.

Measure brand awareness

Brand awareness is at the top of the marketing funnel. Does your market even know you exist? Do they consider you a viable option, or do they prefer your competitors? And most importantly, why? Get the lowdown on how you're perceived and what you need to improve. Use branding and brand identity surveys to diagnose your brand image and build your brand.

Test branding, positioning, and naming

Just do it. Think different. Why do some companies get all the love? Why do loyal customers refuse to be wooed by lower price tags, and choose to stick by their favorite brands? The most revered brands listen to their customers, and tailor their marketing strategies to their target audience. Surveying your customers to test branding and naming concepts will help you understand the attitudes motivations, and preferences of your customers, especially in relation to your competitors.

"Success seems to be connected with action. Successful people keep moving. They make mistakes, but they don't quit." - **Conrad Hilton**

The next chapter shall discuss business plan. I always emphasis on business plan in my books because it is the key and paramount to business start-up, without it your business idea will go down the drain.

CHAPTER FOUR

YOUR BUSINESS PLAN

"A successful man is one who can lay a firm foundation with the bricks that others throw at him." - **David Brinkley**

THIS CHAPTER COVERS:

- Business Plan

You must know that it takes more than a good idea to own a business. Proper planning, creativity and courage to make things happen are required, and you need to be practical as lack of adequate planning often result in a "less than" achievement.

Writing a business plan; of course, you'll need one if you're trying to get any kind of financing, but a business plan is also a great way to test the feasibility of a business idea before you spend a lot of time and money on it.

How to prepare a business plan

What is business plan?

- A business plan is a formal statement containing a set of business goals, alongside the reasons why they are believed to be attainable, and the plan for reaching those goals.
- Contains background information relating to the organization, team or person attempting to reach those goals.
- A business plan can also be described as a document detailing an organization's current status and plans for several years into the future.

- It generally projects future opportunities and act as a roadmap that shows the financial, operational, marketing and strategies that will enable the organization to achieve its goals.

Purpose of a business plan

A business plan is vital for the following reasons:

- Fund- raising
- Entrepreneur/Business owner
- Keeping track/managing performance
- Supporting a company valuation at sale time
- Growth/Expansion/Diversification
- Entering into a partnership business

Benefits of business plan

- ✓ It gives you a sense direction and serves as action plan.
- ✓ Keeps you and your staff focused.
- ✓ Demonstrates the seriousness of your intentions to banks, investors, colleagues and employees.
- ✓ Sets targets and measures your success.
- ✓ Helps you recruit better and higher-level employees.

Also, before you begin to write your business plan, you must determine whether the proposed business plan addresses the following key issues (which basically constitute the initial assessment of the business):

- People
- The opportunity
- The business model
- Strategy
- Context
- Risks and rewards

- Market analysis
- Segmentation
- Market size and growth
- Market trends

Step by step guide of how to write a business plan

A good business plan should be designed to answer the following questions:

- Why does your business exist? (purpose or mission statement)
- Where do you want to take it? (objectives)
- How will it get there? (strategy)
- What will it cost? (budget)

Essential factors that make a good business plan

1. Executive summary
2. General company description

   Normally one to two pages should be adequate for this section. The introductory section should cover:

   - Name of the company, type of legal entity, ownership, significant assets
   - Mission statement of the business
   - Company goals and objectives
   - The main features of the industry in which you will operate
   - The most important company strengths and core competencies
3. The opportunity, industry and market.
4. Strategy
5. Business model
6. Team-management and organization

7. Marketing plan
8. Operational plan
9. Financial plan
10. Appendices

Attributes of a good business plan

*   Make a strong first impression
*   Succinct overview
*   Coherent and complete
*   Focus on financials
*   Business model
*   Promote people
*   Match with mandate
*   Operate plan
*   Marketing plan
*   Layout and presentation of the plan
*   Pitching and presentation the idea

Remember, "It's not what you have; it's what you do with what you have."

Business plan mistakes to avoid

*   Business plan not specific
*   Lack of information about the market
*   Inaccurate finance forecasts
*   You don't know who to ask
*   The plan contains mistakes
*   Lack of a viable opportunity
*   Overestimation of revenues
*   Lack of appreciation for the importance of a good cash flow management
*   Don't create absurdly optimistic "hockey stick projections" of sales taking off in near future
*   Don't exceed 25 pages – don't write too much

- Detailed financial projections should not be excessive
- Minimal use of technical jargon
- Don't forget that "all great achievements require time."

Products and services

1. Product and service description
2. Sourcing
3. Technology
4. Competitive comparison

What type of business plan do I need?

Unsure what kind of business plan you need? Read on.

There are so many different things labelled as business plans; strategic plans, annual plans, operational plans, feasibility plans, and, of course, what most people think of, business plans for start-ups seeking investment. And also, what real business owners want; lean business plans for better management.

I am going to help you figure out which plan is right for you.

Start with this:

Put all business plans into basic principle and knowing an answer to these questions: What do you want your business plan to do for you? That business objective should determine what kind of a plan you need.

We now move to chapter five where we shall view how to grow your business taking cognizance of marketing, branding and record keeping.

CHAPTER FIVE

Part "C"

Sustaining, Growing and Exit plan

Surround yourself with the right people; people who are on the move, focused, determined and ambitious to achieve more!

THIS CHAPTER COVERS:

- Employment
- Marketing and growing the business
- Branding
- Record keeping
- Building a network
- Employment: Hiring the right employee.

As any business owner knows, employees are one of the most important factors in any company. Whether your business is a large multinational organisation or a small start-up that's just beginning to grow, the people you employ are absolutely vital.

For small and medium sized businesses (SMEs) having the right staff can mean the difference between long-term, sustainable success and failure. Larger businesses may be able to cope with staffing hiccups, but these difficulties can have a greater impact on SMEs with fewer resources.

Key to the reputation of your business

One of the major challenges for a start-up business is establishing your reputation – ensuring that your company name is synonymous with good work, quality service and professionalism. With your employees acting as the face of your business, it's vital that you have the right people on-board. It can take years to build a reputation and seconds to destroy one, so it's sensible to put procedures in place to protect the interests of your business and your employees. However even the most dedicated staff can sometimes make mistakes, so it may be advisable to review a range of professional indemnity insurance quotes, to check you have cover should the worst case scenario happens and they make an error.

Key to the future of your business

Not only are the right employees key to keeping clients happy and establishing a lasting reputation, they are also central to a company's internal business culture. In the very early stages of a business, when important protection such as employers liability insurance have been put in place – the first members of staff that you hire are likely to set a precedent, which will be fundamental to the company's ethos and attitude towards its employees in the years to come. Recruiting people that create the desired internal culture early on can help a business to continue to hire 'right-minded' employees for years to come, and this in turn should have a positive effect on the quality of service that your business delivers.

The right employees are vital for any business, whether it's an up-start in the process of arranging its specialist business insurance or a global multi-national firm with thousands of employees worldwide. So, take time over the recruitment process, and think carefully about what your business needs from its employees to ensure lasting success.

In the business world, everyone is paid in two coins: cash and experience. Take the experience first; the cash will come later. – **Harold Geneen**.

Ten tips for hiring an employee?

Hiring the right employee is a challenging process. Hiring the wrong employee is expensive, costly to your work environment, and time consuming. Hiring the right employee, on the other hand, pays you back in employee productivity, a successful employment relationship, and a positive impact on your total work environment.

Hiring the right employee enhances your work culture and pays you back a thousand times over in high employee morale, positive forward thinking planning, and accomplishing challenging goals. This is not a comprehensive guide to hiring, but these steps are key when you hire an employee.

1. Carefully define the job before posting it and recruiting

Hiring the right employee starts with a job analysis. The job analysis enables you to collect information about the duties, responsibilities, necessary skills, outcomes, and work environment of a particular job.

The information from the job analysis is fundamental to developing the job description for the new employee. The job description assists you to plan your recruiting strategy for hiring the right employee.

2. Plan your employee recruiting strategy

With the job description in hand, set up a recruiting planning meeting that involves the key employees who are hiring the new employee. The hiring manager is crucial to the planning. At this meeting, your recruiting strategy is planned and the execution begins. Teams that have worked together frequently in hiring an employee can often complete this step via email.

3. Use a checklist for hiring an employee

This checklist for hiring an employee will help you systematize your process for hiring an employee. Whether it's your first employee or one of many employees you are hiring, this checklist for hiring an employee helps you keep track of your recruiting efforts.

The checklist for hiring an employee keeps your recruiting efforts on track and communicates progress to interested employees and the hiring manager.

4. Recruit the right candidates when hiring an employee

You can develop relationships with potential candidates long before you need them when hiring an employee. These ideas will also help you in recruiting a large pool of candidates when you have a current position available.

The more qualified candidates you can develop when hiring an employee, the more likely you are to locate a qualified potential employee. Read on to discover the best ways to develop your talent pool when hiring an employee.

5. Review credentials and applications carefully

The work of reviewing resumes, cover letters, job applications, and job application letters starts with a well-written job description. Your bulleted list of the most desired characteristics of the most qualified candidate was developed as part of the recruiting planning process.

Screen all applicants against this list of qualifications, skills, experience, and characteristics. You'll be spending your time with your most qualified candidates when hiring an employee. And, that is a good use of your time.

6. Pre-screen candidates by phone when hiring an employee

The most important reason to pre-screen candidates when hiring an employee is to save the interviewing and selection committee time. While a candidate may look good on paper, a pre-screening interview will tell you if their qualifications are truly a fit with your job.

Additionally, in a pre-screening interview, you can determine whether their salary expectations are congruent with your job. A skilled telephone interviewer will also obtain evidence about whether the candidate may fit within your culture or not.

7. Ask the right job interview questions

The job interview is a powerful factor in hiring an employee. The job interview is a key tool employers utilize in hiring. The job interview questions asked are critical in magnifying the power of the job interview to help you in hiring the right employee.

Interview questions that help you separate desirable candidates from average candidates are fundamental when hiring an employee. Job interview questions matter to employers. Here are sample job interview questions.

8. Perform rigorous background checks when hiring an employee

Effective background checks are one of the most important steps when hiring an employee. You need to verify that all the presented, sterling credentials, skills, and experience are actually possessed by your candidate.

The background checks must include work references, especially former supervisors, educational credentials, employment references and actual jobs held, and criminal history. Other background checks when hiring an employee, such as credit history, must be specifically related to the job for which you are hiring an employee.

9. Critical factors to consider before hiring an employee

When you consider hiring an employee, it's tempting to offer the job to the candidate who is most like you. The candidate feels as comfortable as a well-worn shoe. You won't get many surprises once you make the job offer, and your mind is comfortable that your favourite candidate can do the job.

Beware, this practice when hiring an employee. Why does your organization need another employee just like you? Here are the seven critical factors to consider before hiring an employee and making a job offer.

Extend a Job Offer

The job offer letter is provided to the candidate you have selected for the position. Most frequently, the candidate and the organization have verbally negotiated the conditions of hire and the job offer letter confirms the verbal agreements about salary and benefits.

The more senior the position, however, the more likely the job offer will turn into a protracted negotiation about salary, benefits, employment termination, bonus potential, severance pay and more when hiring an employee.

10. Use effective employment letters when hiring an employee

These sample employment letters will assist you to reject job candidates, make job offers, welcome employees, and more when hiring an employee. Use these sample employment letters to develop the employment letters you use in your organization when hiring an employee.

"An exceptionally knowledgeable person with his deep knowledge of wide ranging subjects has the capability to provide solutions to almost every problem. He has the intelligence required to understand the basic nature of the problem and then work accordingly towards finding it's solution. He always gives right advice to the right people at the right time". - **Sam Veda**

Let us now take a look at marketing and growing the business for good business sustainability

Marketing and Growing the Business

Marketing takes time, money, and lots of preparation. One of the best ways to prepare yourself is to develop a solid marketing plan. A strong marketing plan will ensure you're not only sticking to your schedule, but that you are spending your marketing funds wisely and appropriately. Below is how to develop a marketing plan that will grow the business.

Developing a Marketing Plan that will grow the Business

A marketing plan includes everything from understanding your target market and your competitive position in that market, to how you intend to reach that market (your tactics) and differentiate yourself from your competition in order to make a sale.

Your small business marketing budget should be a component of your marketing plan. Essentially, it will outline the costs of how you are going to achieve your marketing goals within a certain timeframe.

If you don't have the funds to hire a marketing firm or even staff a position in-house, there are resources available to guide you through the process of writing a marketing plan and developing a market budget.

Bend Your Budget When Necessary and Keep an Eye on ROI

Once you have developed your marketing budget, it doesn't mean that it is set in stone. There may be times when you need to throw in another unplanned marketing tactic; such as hosting an event or creating a newspaper ad - to help you reach your market more effectively.

Ultimately, it's more important to determine whether sticking to your budget is helping you achieve your marketing goals and bringing you a return on investment (ROI) than to adhere to a rigid and fixed budget.

That's why it's important to include a plan for measuring your spend. Consider what impact certain marketing activities have had on your revenues during a fixed period, such as a business quarter, compared to another time period when you focused your efforts on other tactics. Consider the tactics that worked as well as those that didn't work. You don't have to cut the tactics that didn't work, but you should assess whether you need to give them more time to work or whether the funds are best redirected elsewhere.

Marketing plans should be maintained on an annual basis, at a minimum. But if you launch a new product or service, take time to revisit your original plan or develop a separate campaign plan that you can add to your main plan as an addendum.

At the end of the day, the time spent developing your marketing plan, is time well spent because it defines how you connect with your customers. And that's an investment worth making. The next is branding.

Branding

The American Marketing Association (AMA) defines a brand as a "name, term, sign, symbol or design, or a combination of them intended to identify the goods and services of one seller or group of sellers and to differentiate them from those of other sellers.

Therefore it makes sense to understand that branding is not about getting your target market to choose you over the competition, but it is about getting your prospects to see you as the only one that provides a solution to their problem.

The objectives that a good brand will achieve include:

- Delivers the message clearly
- Confirms your credibility
- Connects your target prospects emotionally
- Motivates the buyer
- Concretes user loyalty

To succeed in branding, you must understand the needs and wants of your customers and prospects. You do this by integrating your brand strategies through your company at every point of public contact. You now consider Record keeping.

Recordkeeping

Why should I keep records?

Good records will help you monitor the progress of your business, prepare your financial statements, identify sources of income, keep track of deductible expenses, keep track of your basis in property, prepare your tax returns, and support items reported on your tax returns.

What kinds of records should I keep?

You may choose any recordkeeping system suited to your business that clearly shows your income and expenses. Except in a few cases, the law does not require any special kind of records. However, the law requires a proper financial record should be kept, business you are in affects the type of records you need to keep for federal tax purposes.

How long should I keep records?

The length of time you should keep a document depends on the action, expense, or the type of document records. You must keep your records as long as needed to prove the income or deductions on a tax return.

How should I record my business transactions?

Purchases, sales, payroll, and other transactions you have in your business generate supporting documents. These documents contain information you need to record in your books.

What is the burden of proof?

The responsibility to substantiate entries, deductions, and statements made on your tax returns is known as the burden of proof. You must be able to prove certain elements of expenses to deduct them.

How long should I keep employment tax records?

Keep all records of employment taxes for at least four years.

Next is building a network.

Building a Network

Want to make your business networking more effective? Here are tips to keep in mind. Effective business networking is the linking together of individuals who, through trust and relationship building, become walking, talking advertisements for one another.

Business networking is an effective low-cost marketing method for developing sales opportunities and contacts, based on referrals and introductions either face-to-face at meetings and gatherings, or by other contact methods such as phone, email, and increasingly social and business networking websites.

1. **Win friends and allies**
2. **Meet new people with confidence**
3. **Build valuable relationships**
4. **Get people to help you in networking your business**
5. **Build your profile**

A good network is created, and networking succeeds, by the application of hard work. A network without the work produces nothing worthwhile.

The exit plans

Transferring the business to the next generation

What it takes

A successful business is not only one that rakes in a sizable profit regularly, but one that has survived the founder. Ensuring the longevity of a business from start up to transfer from generation to generation is built around planning. Planning and more planning for the success and succession of your business is critical to giving it an increased opportunity to thrive into and through the next generation.

Two major aspects to ensuring the smooth transition of a business from one generation to another includes; first, plans to make sure the people, to whom the business is being passed on to, are ready. Secondly, plans to make sure the business would make it through the generation to which it is being passed on to and make it successfully to the next generation of leaders.

Planning the people

Planning for succession includes recognizing and celebrating small breakthroughs as they come as well as getting documents in order to guide the transition process in case of death or transfer. The planning also includes tactically thinking about how best to grow and position the business for on-going success especially in a highly competitive market. Taking the time to assess where the business currently is, determining where you want it to get to in a certain number of years and outlining the goals and action steps that can be taken to achieve this. This does not have to be a long drawn out process but it does need to be clear and relevant.

Succession planning is about the people most of all. The business you are building and which you plan to leave for the next generation needs human beings not machinery to operate it. The people taking on leadership need a path forward and the knowledge, skills and abilities to successfully take the baton from the outgoing leadership. Taking the time to assess the strengths and weaknesses of potential new leaders and then creating a successor development plan for them, is powerful. Businesses that put the effort into developing people experience a process of continued growth as they grow new leaders prior to the time when they take on the full mantle of responsibility. The planning, people, and provision for success are critical elements in every succession plan.

Planning the Systems and Strategies

The provision of exit strategies, business structures and funding that effectively prepare the business to move successfully through the next generation can make or break the legacy you are building. Over time businesses typically grow in size and value. This growth presents challenges and opportunities. Take the time to carefully plan for what that growth will look like so that the next generation can exit the business to make room for successors. This means making sure the exit strategies do not drain the business or leave it weakened in some way. Paying attention to business structures to minimize transition difficulties and tax liabilities can make or break a business. Desire to pass a business on to the next generation is one thing, providing the funding and economic viability is another. How will the successor generations be able to take on the business without compromising the lifestyle of the outgoing business leaders? In planning, people and provision for success are critical elements in every succession plan. Taking the time to cultivate success will go a long way to grow your business now and through the next generation.

While planning for the succession of a company, issues like inheritance tax, legal issues and 'the will' if there is any, are taken into consideration to ensure a smooth transition as well as the proper documentation required by the new management.

The Steps and How: Succession of Your Business

Step 1: Determine what's important to you: Unless you know what's important to you and your family, you can't make sound decisions that will impact future generations. That's why the first step is to recognize what your family's core values are and how your positive family heritage has led to the success you enjoy today. Some questions to consider are: "Who was the most influential person in your life between ages 10-15 and why?" "What challenges have you overcome, and what traits got you through it?" "What does an abundant life mean to you?" and "What three things would you want your great-grandchildren to know about you?" You may be surprised to hear your own answers. But by uncovering what has impacted you in the past, as well as what you envision for your future, you can see patterns emerge that can help guide your succession planning process.

Step 2: Create your family's vision statement: Once you've determined what's important to your family, you can create your family's vision statement. This is usually a four-to-ten-page document designed to unify and preserve the family by articulating what's most important to you. Think of the vision statement as a guiding light for children, grandchildren, and future generations; helping them understand their unique family heritage and positively influencing them to live fulfilling, meaningful lives. To supplement the vision statement, you can also create a video of the family history, where each parent and/or grandparent "tells their story" so it can be passed on to future generations.

Step 3: Hold a family meeting: No matter how well you articulate your family vision statement, it can't do its job if it isn't properly presented to family members. By answering a series of highly targeted questions, such as, "If you received a check from your parents for $100,000 today, what would you do with it?" and "How have you seen your parents demonstrate the values described in the vision statement?" your heirs will be guided to self-discover the power and value of the family vision statement. Remember, you can't force your heirs to live lives of significance. In fact, the harder you try to tell them "what's good for them," the greater they will resist. Therefore, they will need to be guided to discover on their own the value of, and personal benefits to them, of the family vision statement.

Step 4: Create a family council: The family council is a powerful tool to help build family unity and cohesiveness through a shared vision of the family's purpose. Family members are given specific duties and responsibilities, such as investigating how to invest family money together, identifying those charities and causes that best align with the family's values, setting up future family council meetings, and establishing a budget and agenda, which requires engagement with other family members to accomplish their goals. Ultimately, the family council serves as a repository for all the experience, connections, education, know-how, business and people skills the family has acquired over the generations.

Step 5: Get your team involved: Now that you know what matters most to your family and everyone is on the same page, you need to keep your attorney, CPA, stockbroker, insurance agent, and anyone else assisting with your family business succession plan abreast of your desires. Armed with a copy of your family vision statement, these various professionals can help turn your desires into reality by using their unique skills to create strategies, tactics and tools designed to bring your vision statement to life. Realize, though, that this concept of "family first" may seem foreign and unnecessary to some of your advisors, as their focus is tax savings and legal strategies, not matters of the heart. Let us see inheritance.

Inheritance

Passing on a family business is important but maintaining the legacy is more important. There should be proper rules guiding the family and the business in term of setting a model of resolving conflict, selection of successor and head of the business, death and replacement, structuring regular meetings,

The Stand of Law to Inheritance

In law, an *heir* is a person who is entitled to receive a share of the deceased's (the person who died) property, subject to the rules of inheritance in the jurisdiction where the deceased (decedent) died or owned property at the time of death. A person does not become an heir before the death of the deceased, since the exact identity of the persons entitled to inherit is determined only then. Members of ruling noble or royal houses expected to become heirs are called heirs apparent if first in line and incapable of being displaced from inheriting by another claim; otherwise, they are heirs presumptive. There is a further concept of joint inheritance, pending renunciation by all but one, which is called coparceny.

In modern law, the terms *inheritance* and *heir* refer exclusively to succession to property by descent from a deceased dying intestate. Takers in property succeeded to under a will are termed generally *beneficiaries,* and specifically *devisees* for real property, *bequests* for personal property, or *legatees* for money.

In the case of passing inheritance in form of family business to the heir, there will set down rules that will guide the selection of heir, especially in case of multiple heir.

Dealing with Family Discord

Whether it's a difference of opinion or a performance issue, dealing with discord or conflict among family members in a business environment is tough.

Families will always bicker, but the challenge is preventing the bickering from interfering with the business and rubbing-off on non-family employees who might be tempted to use the same emotional appeal to gain position or get their own way – because they've seen your family succeed at it.

Especially challenging is trying to remain objective about the situation. Try not to take sides with any particular family member, and make it known that you won't let disagreements affect your business. This not only stops disruptive family members from using emotions to politick for status – it also sends a clear message to other employees.

If you find yourself stuck with a difficult family employee with whom you can't reconcile yourself, consider moving them into a new line of work or encourage them to transfer to another branch.

Preparing the Next Generation

Many family businesses remain so for years if not decades, but how do you ensure that the next generation continues to grow your business and serve your loyal customers when you come to retire or move-on?

The best time to plan for succession is well in advance! As invested family members, consider these questions:

- What are your family goals for the future?
- What are the plans of the next generation?

- Who is interested in staying in business and leading the way? Is there more than one aspiring leader-in-the-works?
- Who is best equipped to lead? What role will the other members play?
- And, of course, what if no one is interested in succeeding your business?

Then develop a plan to groom and mentor the future leader(s) of your business. Set a goal for the transition to begin, take it slowly so that you can still have a part-time hand in your business and provide on-the-job mentoring, without being too much of a micro-manager.

You'll also need to plan the financial and legal steps of transferring business ownership. SBA offers guidance on the steps you'll need to exiting a business.

The next chapter covers things to avoid when starting a business. The essence is to guide you from making mistakes that can lead to business failure.

CHAPTER SIX

THE THINGS TO AVOID

If you don't drive your business, you will be driven out of business. –
B. C. Forbes

THIS CHAPTER COVERS:

- Things to avoid when running a business

Starting a new business is a simple issue or complicated, depending
on the way one looks at it. If one finds it cumbersome, it is best that
it is avoided and continued with a more comfortable nine-to-five.
Starting a business is simple for self-motivated people, but
irrespective of motivation there are certain things that one should
avoid while embarking on their path to financial freedom.

Things to avoid when running a business

There's no such thing as an overnight success story when it comes to
businesses—even if a company appears to have just stumbled upon a
great product that the world is clamouring for, you can bet that there
was a lot of hard work and planning behind the scenes. If you decide
to start your own business, don't assume it's going to be all smooth
sailing with minimal work. Here are 10 things you need to avoid
when running a business:

1. **Procrastinating on your business plan.** You need a
   business plan before you even start your business so that you
   know your goals, your target market, and what sets you apart

from the competition. Oh, and your business plan isn't done once you write it—it should continue to evolve along with your business.

2. **Hiring too many people too quickly.** When you're first starting out, you're probably not going to have the budget to hire as many people as you would like to handle the day-to-day tasks that you don't want to do. You'll need to be prepared to get used to the responsibilities of your business so that when you can afford to hire, you hire the people who will be best suited to handle the work.

3. **Being unwilling to delegate.** While you don't want to get carried away with bringing on staff, you also shouldn't feel as if you have to do everything yourself. Even if you're not ready to bring on a full-time employee, consider working on a per-project basis with freelancers to accomplish things like designing your logo and setting up your website.

4. **Racking up too many overhead costs.** It may be true that you have to spend money to make money, but you still have to draw the line somewhere when it comes to spending. You'll want to establish early on what overhead costs are essential to your business and what costs are superfluous. For example, if you run an online business, you might be able to operate out of your home at first rather than renting an office.

5. **Failing to know the target customers.** If you don't understand who is going to buy your product, how are you ever

going to reach out to leads and run marketing campaigns? Do your market research to determine what demographics most need or want your product.

6. **Making customers feel unappreciated.** Retaining loyal customers is significantly less expensive than attracting new customers, so don't forget to nourish existing relationships. Offer loyal customers special deals or personalized attention to make them feel valued.

7. **Failing to know the competition.** You won't be able to fully differentiate yourself from your competition unless you know who your competition is. Do some research and figure out what sets your business apart so that you can emphasize your advantages in your marketing. And if you discover that the market is already saturated, you'll need to figure out how to pivot and offer something distinct from the former competition.

8. **Failing to understand what you're selling.** One of the biggest mistakes businesses make in marketing their products or services is focusing on the specific features rather than what those features will do for the consumer. Your customers want to know what's in it for them, not just what you've been labouring over.

9. **Putting online marketing on the back burner.** Ignoring online marketing can be a fatal mistake for the modern business. With smartphones becoming increasingly popular and accessible, more and more people are primarily learning about

businesses by going online. If they can't easily find you through a Google search, you can guarantee that they'll be able to find one or more of your competitors.

10. **Not investing in any marketing.** Sure, you probably don't want to be spending all your money on expensive TV spots when you first start, but you should be focusing on less expensive forms of marketing, such as creating a blog, putting on a local live event, or encouraging tastemakers to promote your products.

We now enter the next chapter where we shall be discussing cash flow, the life wire of every business.

CHAPTER SEVEN

CASH FLOW

Number one cash is the king… number two, communicate… number three buy or bury the competition. - **Jack Welch**

THIS CHAPTER COVERS:

- The effect of cash flow in business
- Components of cash flow
- Cash flow analysis

Liquid cash is the heartbeat of every business which needs to keep pumping the blood to the system to keep it alive. Cash flow is the amount of net cash generated by an investment or a business during a specific period. One measure of cash flow is earning before interest, taxes, depreciation and amortization, because cash is fuel that drive a business, many analysts consider cashflow to be a company's most important financial statistic. Firm with big cashflows are frequently takeover targets because acquiring firms know that the cash can be used to help pay off the costs of the acquisitions.

Cashflow is a measure of changes in a company's cash account during an accounting period, specially its cash income minus the cash payments it makes.

The effect of Cash Flow in business

A typical business budget, projects your total income and expenses, often averaging the amounts per month, rather than recording when they actually occur. Cash flow relates to the timing of when money comes in and expenses are due. It's important to track cash flow because even if you make adequate sales to cover your expenses and return a profit, you might experience financial, production and credit problems if your customers don't pay you in a timely manner.

If you make a sale and offer 90-day terms but have to pay your suppliers within 30 days for the materials you used to create the product for that sale, you have not planned your cash flow efficiently. Creating a cash flow budget in addition to your master budget can help you plan your financial needs. For example, if you pay quarterly machinery lease payments of $600, you might budget $200 per month in your master budget to show your average monthly operating costs for the year. A cash flow budget shows that you will have to make $600 payments in four specific months.

Production and Sales Interruptions

If you don't plan your cash flow well, you won't have enough money to pay your bills on time, possibly resulting in the need to shut down production because you can't get materials or pay your workers. When you can't meet customer demand, you may lose orders or customers permanently. In addition to losing business, you might have to forgo new business opportunities because you can't buy materials or hire workers to fulfil orders.

Credit Damage

Without enough cash on hand to pay your bills or make debt payments, such as on credit cards or loans, you can damage your credit. In addition to having businesses, credit card companies or banks report you to credit agencies, your credit score can go down, resulting in higher interest rates or denials on future loans.

Considerations

You can improve cash flow by negotiating better credit terms with lenders and suppliers, making more cash sales, tightening your credit terms with customers and keeping cash reserves on hand for unexpected situations. During critical cash flow periods, consider selling your receivables to a factor to get needed cash to continue operating. A factor is a person or company that buys receivables, at a discount, letting you get cash quicker and allowing the factor to make a profit. Temporary negative cash flow is not a bad thing. For example, if you have $10,000 more in expenses than income in January but $30,000 positive cash flow in February, your overall cash flow situation is positive.

Components of Cash Flow

The cash flow for a company includes three parts:

1. **Operating cash flow**: It refers to the cash received or loss because of the internal activities of a company such as the cash received from sales revenue or the cash paid to the workers.
2. **Investment cash flow**: It refers to the cash flow which related to the company's non-current asset such as equipment building and so on such as the cash used to buy new equipment or a building.
3. **Financing cash flow**: cash flow from a company's financing activities like issuing stock or paying dividends.

The sum of the three components above will be the **total cash flow** of a company.

Examples

Description	Amount ($)	totals ($)
Cash flow from operations		**+70**
Sales (paid in cash)	+30	
Incoming loan	+50	
Loan repayment	-5	
Taxes	-5	
Cash flow from investments		**-10**
Purchased capital	-10	
Total		**60**

The net cash flow only provides a limited amount of information. Compare, for instance, the cash flows over three years of two companies:

	Company A			Company B		
	Year 1	Year 2	year 3	Year 1	Year 2	year 3
Cash flow from operations	+20M	+21M	+22M	+10M	+11M	+12M
Cash flow from financing	+5M	+5M	+5M	+5M	+5M	+5M
Cash flow from investment	-15M	-15M	-15M	0M	0M	0M
Net cash flow	+10M	+11M	+12M	+15M	+16M	+17M

Company B has a higher yearly cash flow. However, Company A is actually earning more cash by its core activities and has already spent 45M in long term investments, of which the revenues will only show up after three years.

Cash Flow Analysis

Cash flows are often transformed into measures that give information e.g. on a company's value and situation:

- To determine a project's rate of return or value. The time of cash flows into and out of projects are used as inputs in financial models such as internal rate of return and net present value.
- To determine problems with a business's liquidity. Being profitable does not necessarily mean being liquid. A company can fail because of a shortage of cash even while profitable.

- As an alternative measure of a business's profits when it is believed that accrual accounting concepts do not represent economic realities. For instance, a company may be notionally profitable but generating little operational cash (as may be the case for a company that barters its products rather than selling for cash). In such a case, the company may be deriving additional operating cash by issuing shares or raising additional debt finance.
- Cash flow can be used to evaluate the 'quality' of income generated by accrual accounting. When net income is composed of large non-cash items it is considered low quality.
- To evaluate the risks within a financial product, e.g., matching cash requirements, evaluating default risk, re-investment requirements, etc.

Cash flow notion is based loosely on cash flow statement accounting standards. The term is flexible and can refer to time intervals spanning over past-future. It can refer to the total of all flows involved or a subset of those flows. Subset terms include net cash flow, operating cash flow and free cash flow.

Case study:

Financial analysts generally consider cash flow to be best measure of a company's financial health. Increased cash flow means more funds are available to pay dividends, service or reduce debt and invest in new assets. On the other hand, reported net income is heavily influenced by firm's accounting practices. Reduced income generally means lower taxes and more cash, thus the same accounting practices that reduce net income can actually increase cash flow. A firm with large amount of new investment and corresponding high depreciation charges might report low or negative earnings at the same time it has large cash flows to service debt and to acquire additional assets.

Cable companies have huge investment requirements and are typical of firms that may be quite healthy in spite of reporting net losses. In early 1996, TCI communications, at the time the nation's largest cable operator, reported fourth-quarter result that included a net loss of $70 million, more than double the loss reported in the year-earlier quarter. At the same time the firm added more than a million new customers and reported a 5% increase in cashflow. Thus, although TCI reported an additional loss, the first quarter was generally considered quite successful.

Symptoms of cash flow problems

There are many reasons a business can suffer cash flow problems – some are down to mismanagement and poor decisions, and in some cases factors outside of your control. Any of the following symptoms can indicate that a business is experiencing cash flow problems:

- Up to overdraft limit – no headroom / returned payments
- Stretch to pay salaries each month
- Trade creditor arrears
- Taxation arrears
- Rent arrears
- No working capital 'buffer' – surviving day to day
- Negative working capital on balance sheet – over geared / losses?
- Lack of funds for remedial action (redundancies / premises relocation)
- Lack of profitability – insufficient to support owner / manager's lifestyle
- Unable to pay for professional advice

"The real test is not whether you avoid this failure, because you won't. It's whether you let it harden or shame you into inaction, or whether you learn from it; whether you choose to persevere." -
Barack Obama

CONCLUSION

Final thoughts

Starting and running your own business will be the most exciting, rewarding and fulfilling work you can ever do, though, for it to be a success, it requires a lot of commitment, courage, hard work, consistency and creativity, but the reward is worthwhile. Never give up, even though so much can go wrong, it is your sole responsibility to make it go right, learn from your mistakes to make things work. Keep walking toward perfection in your products or services in order to beat your customers' expectation, the result of this will not only earn you business recognition and good reputation, but will also provide you with a lifestyle that you have always aspire.

If you strictly follow the instructions and principles in this book, that is; focus on what you need to do before you start your own business, how to start the business and how to sustain the business and keep it running – you will not only successfully build a business but also become a business you, your staff and your customers are proud of. G. K. Chesterton said, "I owe my success to having listened respectfully to the very best advice, and then going away and doing the exact opposite." Bad advice is costly, but good advice brings wealth, abundance and success. The principles in this book are good advice!

Remember, before you start; no matter how small you want to start, you must look at the big picture, how you expect the business to be in five, ten or twenty years and work toward it, be determined and be focused, do not let any obstacle bring you down but rather use each stumbling block to project the business.

"Don't let the fear of losing be greater than the excitement of winning." - **Robert Kiyosaki**.

How to start: Converting your business idea to reality needs creativity and determination. Ensure you build a plan that will test the feasibility of a business idea before you spend a lot of time and money on it. Market research also is a good indicator of where you need to go next with your idea.

You must have it in mind that sustaining and growing the business requires commitment in doing the right thing, and also knowing what to avoid in business. There are many things to avoid in business in order to maintain smooth running and growth, and also important things you must ensure are in place to sustain the business.

"We've demonstrated a strong track record of being very disciplined with the use of our cash. We don't let it burn a hole in our pocket, we don't allow it to motivate us to do stupid acquisitions. And so, I think that we'd like to continue to keep our powder dry, because we do feel that there are one or more strategic opportunities in the future"
- Steve Jobs

This book will help you achieve the three 'M's':
1. Make you a business owner
2. Mature your business to standard
3. Multiply your business and your reward

If you need help in turning your business idea into a business success, email me at info@peterosalor.org.

I wish you all the best of success in your business journeys!

TO GOD BE THE GLORY.

APPENDIX

26 principles for business success

Below is a list of 26 principles I've developed to stay true to what is important. The principles will guild you on what you have learnt in this book, and are a foundation for all of the necessary principles required to have a successful business. The list serves as a reminder, and will keep you on track if you refer to it frequently and follow it. You will get the best results from the list if you keep it posted somewhere you can see it every day.

1. Life may be a banquet, but we must understand that there is no free lunch.

2. There is no need to develop rigid goals unless we wish to greatly underachieve our potential.

3. Become a disciplined manager of your time use, always focusing on the highest priority in your life at that moment.

4. No statue was ever erected to a critic. Think long and hard before you speak harsh words about someone or something.

5. Don't try to change everyone around you. Try changing yourself!

6. Study every aspect on leadership that you can, because life is about either leading yourself or leading others.

7. What to learn about success? Try hanging around successful people and implementing what they teach you.

8. Jobs have a limited future. A career is an open-ended opportunity.

9. Make it a rule to learn something new every day.

10. Winners understand they must avoid doing the things failures do.

11. Being disciplined opens doors to the greater opportunities of life. Not being disciplined closes these same doors, trapping us in the world of unfulfilled opportunities.

12. A lack of adequate planning often results in a "less than" achievement.

13. Inertia grounds our momentum. Taking action is how we start momentum.

14. Never underestimate the vastness of your experiences. Use them to help you grasp new opportunities in your career. Experience can be the great equalizer in a very competitive world.

15. Don't spend time worrying about what you don't have. Instead, focus on what you want life to bring you and work like hell to make that your reality.

16. Goals create a foundation upon which to build your house of success.

17. Make saving a part of every dollar you earn. Make giving a portion of every dollar you earn to worthy causes.

18. The biggest internal struggle many have is to keep their "darkest secrets" out of the light of day. Instead, we must forgive ourselves as God is willing to forgive us and turn our darkness into glowing rays of light.

19. Most of life's fears are a needless waste of energy.

20. Learn to see possibilities, not liabilities, by dwelling on what can be rather than on what cannot be.

21. Keep the right priorities of life in this order: God, family, career.

22. Honesty, integrity promise-keeping, trustworthiness and loyalty must be the content of your character.

23. Excellent customer service and good selling skills is the key to business success.

24. Accountability must be your order of the day.

25. Have a good banking relationship and strong cash position

26. Have respect for the laws of the land.

REFERENCES

- *Yuliya Franklin, director of Key Entrepreneur Development Center at Corporate College, a division of Cuyahoga Community College.*

- *The Advantages and Disadvantages of Owning Your Own company by Rose Johnson, Demand Media*

- *The Advantages and Disadvantages of Owning Your Own Business by Malcolm Orchard.*

- ***Karen E. Spaede*** *(*How to Research Your Business Idea*).*

- Aaron Keller, Nancy A. Shenker, president of the ONswitch LLC.. Pali Rao, Jacob Wackerhausen, Steve Cole, Jacob Wackerhausen, Lisa F. Young, Monika Wisniewska, BigStockPhoto.com, by Stephanie Speisman, Joe Daley - Founder of **Logomyway.com.**

- Sam Ashe-Edmunds (The effect of Cash Flow in Business). Wall Street Words: An A to Z Guide to Investment Terms for Today's Investor by David L. Scott.

BOOKS BY THE AUTHOR

Peter Osalor FCCA CTA

WHY AND HOW TO START YOUR OWN BUSINESS
A Simple Guide for Business Start-ups

Peter Osalor FCCA CTA

HOW TO PREPARE A BUSINESS PLAN
A Step by Step Guide

Peter Osalor FCCA CTA

HOW TO IDENTIFY AND FUND YOUR BUSINESS
200 Business Ideas and 28 Ways to Raise Capital for Your Business

Peter Osalor FCCA CTA

SUCCESS IN YOUR BUSINESS
HOW TO BECOME A SUCCESSFUL ENTREPRENEUR

Peter Osalor *FCCA CTA*

The
Entrepreneurial
Revolution
A solution for poverty eradication

Peter Osalor FCCA, CTA

ECONOMIC
TRANSFORMATION
From a Poor Person to a Wealthy Person,
From a Poor Nation to a Wealthy Nation

Entrepreneur, Entrepreneurship, Entrepreneualism,
MSME, Entrepreneurial Revolution

50 Proven
Cures
For Poverty

Entrepreneurs, Entreprepreneurialism
and the Free Market

150
Barristers
YOU
CAN DO!

Time tested
principles for
transforming
your
environment

Peter Osalor

Peter Osalor FCCA CTA
Harry Koranteng FCCA ACMA

DO IT YOURSELF (UK)
SELF-ASSESSMENT
TAX RETURNS FOR
NON-ACCOUNTANTS

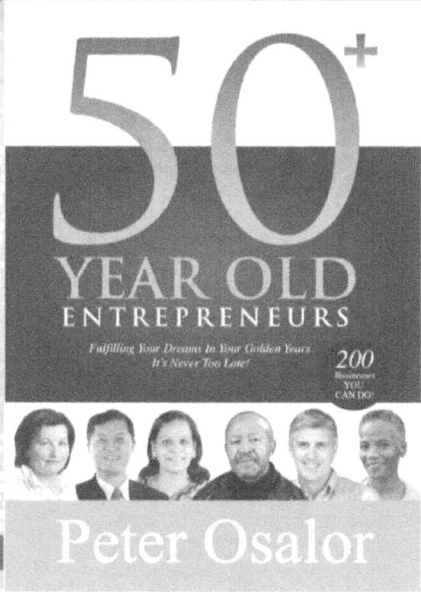

BECOME WEALTHY

CREATE MORE THAN ONE SOURCE OF INCOME AND MOVE OUT OF POVERTY

PETER OSALOR FCCA, CTA

START A BUSINESS

The A to Z of Starting & Running a Successful Business!

PETER OSALOR FCCA, CTA

BUSINESS BUILDING

HOW TO BUILD A BUSINESS THAT OUTLIVES YOU!

PETER OSALOR FCCA, CTA

START SMALL AND GROW BIG

MSMES (Micro small and Medium size Enterprises) Revolution

steps!
small
journeys
start with
big

Peter Osalor FCCA, CTA

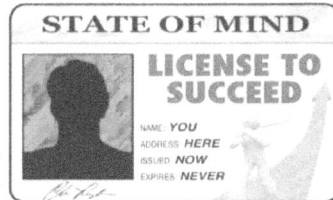

From the author of *Success In Your Business Series*

The **Thinking** of an
Entrepreneur

PETER OSALOR FCCA, CTA

The
Farmer
Entrepreneur

A practical guide to Agri-business

Peter Osalor

Made in United States
Cleveland, OH
24 June 2025

17964790R00056